Splashy Fins, Flashy Skins: Deep-Sea Rhymes To Make You Grin

*To Anja, the real fish
lover in the family.*

*Thank you to Dolly
Howard at the Keene
Public Library for her
valuable research
assistance.*

Cover photograph © 2002 Norbert Wu/www.norbertwu.com

Photographs courtesy of © 2002 Norbert Wu/www.norbertwu.com
Other photographs courtesy of Photo Researchers, Inc.: pp. 16-17 (© Andrew
J. Martinez), 24-25 (© Tom McHugh); ©1994 Breton Cole/Mo Yung
Productions: p. 25 (right)

Published by The Millbrook Press
2 Old New Milford Road
Brookfield, CT 06804

Library of Congress Cataloging-in-Publication Data

Copeland, Cynthia L.
  Splashy fins, flashy skins : deep-sea rhymes to make you grin /
Cynthia L. Copeland, Alexandra P. Lewis.
      p. cm. — (Silly Millies)
Summary: Illustrations and easy text point out strange physical
characteristics or behaviors of certain ocean fish, such as hagfish,
unicornfish, and frogfish.
  ISBN 0-7613-2906-4 (lib. bdg.)   ISBN 0-7613-1830-5 (pbk.)
  [1. Fishes—Fiction.] I. Lewis, Alexandra P. II. Title. III. Silly
Millies.
  PZ7.C78797 Sp 2003
  [Fic]—dc21
                                    2002012374

5 4 3 2 1 (lib.)
5 4 3 2 1 (pbk.)

silly Millies

Splashy Fins, Flashy Skins: Deep-Sea Rhymes To Make You Grin

Cynthia L. Copeland   Alexandra P. Lewis

The Millbrook Press
Brookfield, Connecticut

So many creatures in the sea . . .

Blue spot Stingray

Oriental Sweetlips

Napoleon wrasse

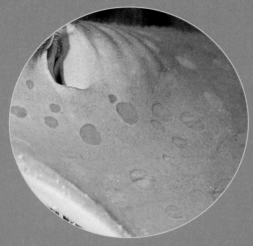

. . . dotted,

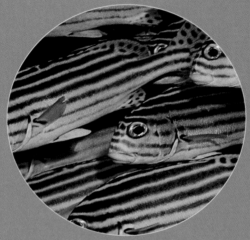

striped,

and zigzaggy.

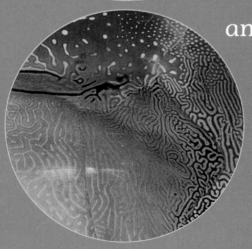

Scallop

Some creatures have
a lot of eyes,
some have a
lot of legs.

Arrow crab

Some swim around with their
bellies full of lots of little eggs.

Sea horse

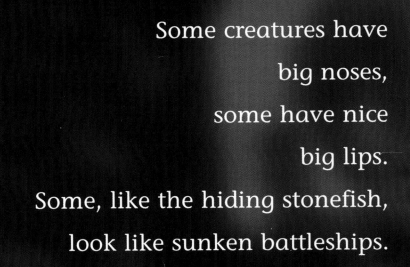

Some creatures have
big noses,
some have nice
big lips.
Some, like the hiding stonefish,
look like sunken battleships.

Red-lipped Batfish

Blue Grouper

Stonefish

Puffer fish is a deep-sea fake,
he is usually flat, not fat.

Puffer fish

But when the big fish follow him
(the ones who want to swallow him),
he puffs up and stays that way,
so they will not eat him today!

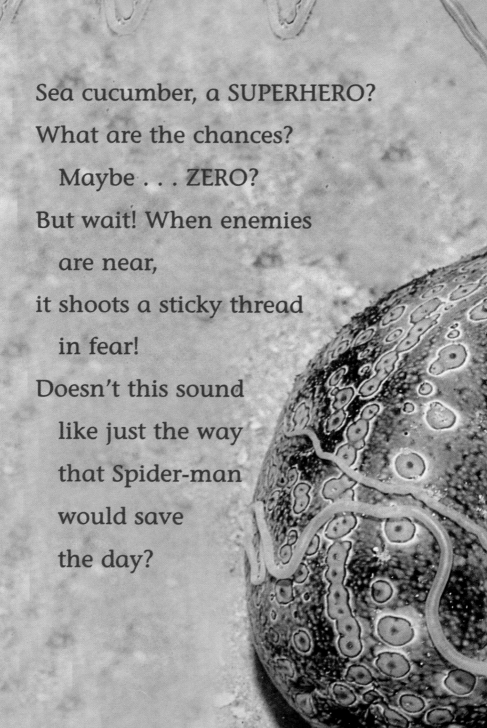

Sea cucumber, a SUPERHERO?
What are the chances?
    Maybe . . . ZERO?
But wait! When enemies
    are near,
it shoots a sticky thread
    in fear!
Doesn't this sound
    like just the way
    that Spider-man
    would save
    the day?

Sea Cucumber

Anglerfish

I am an anglerfish.

I fish for me.

I fish at the bottom of

the deep dark sea.

My bait is a rod

at the end of my nose.

Come closer, little fish.

My jaws open

and . . . CLOSE!

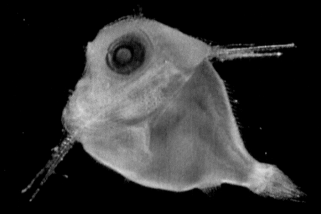

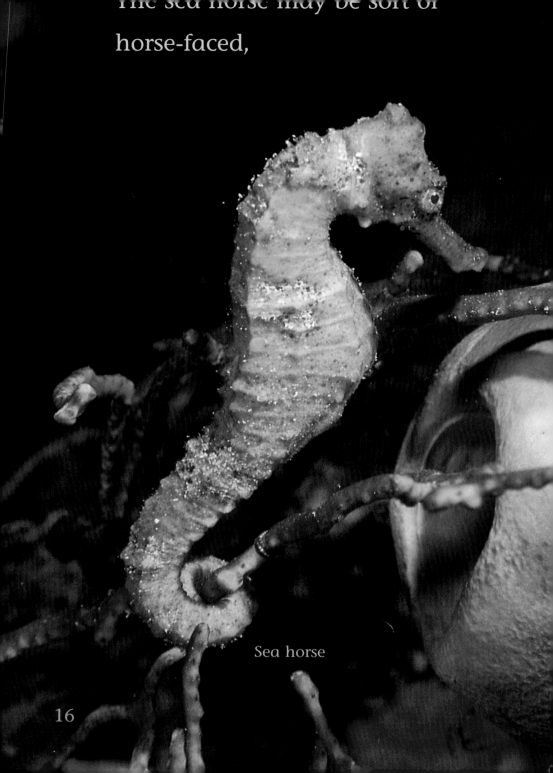

The sea horse may be sort of
horse-faced,

Sea horse

but all four legs have been erased!
The seahorse does not even swim,
he waits for food to come to him.
And the only way to ride this horse,
is to close your eyes and dream,
of course.

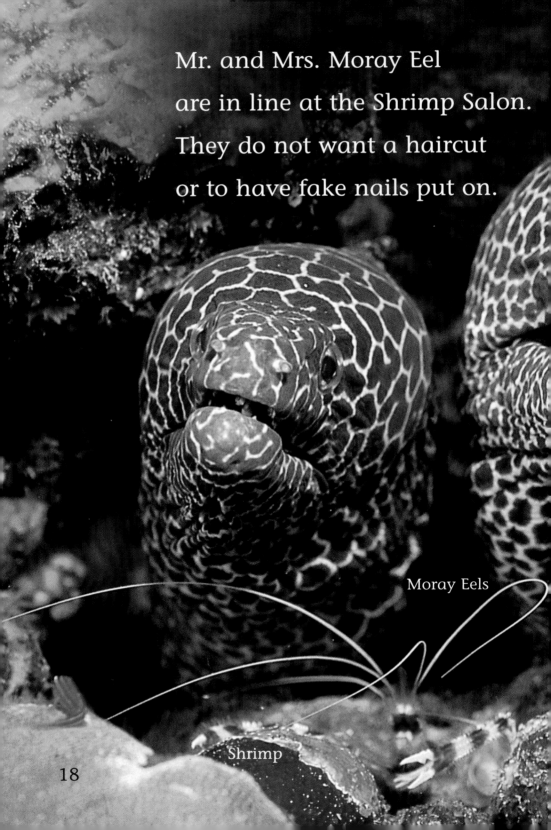

Mr. and Mrs. Moray Eel
are in line at the Shrimp Salon.
They do not want a haircut
or to have fake nails put on.

Moray Eels

Shrimp

18

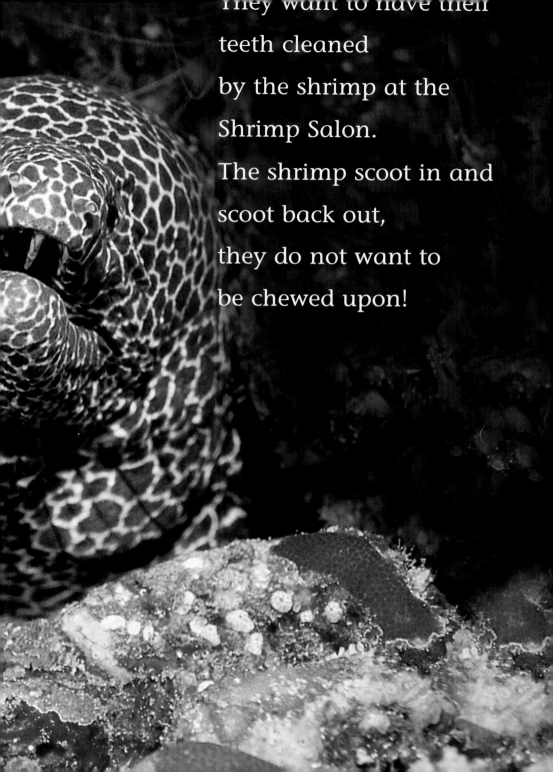

They want to have their
teeth cleaned
by the shrimp at the
Shrimp Salon.
The shrimp scoot in and
scoot back out,
they do not want to
be chewed upon!

A fish out of water?

How can that be?

Mudskipper forgot he belongs

in the sea!

With fins for feet,

he can crawl and creep

and look for tasty things to eat!

Mudskipper

Frogfish

Here is a . . .
lumpy,
bumpy
frogfish.

She is . . .
hiding
gliding,
and deciding . . .

which little swishy,
sweet-tasting fishy,
will be her
dinner dish-y!

The hagfish has a clever
way to keep from
being someone's prey.
When scared,

Hagfish

he uses

the slime

he oozes

to hide himself away.

In fables and in fairy tales,
the unicorn with the single horn
is a myth, a made-up beast.
But the unicorn fish
is more than wish

or whimsy—he is real!
When he swims he uses his horn
to poke and prod and feel.

Unicorn fish

This fish is very scary.

Hatchetfish

This looks like a fairy.

Leafy Sea Dragon

The cowfish wants a kiss good-bye.
The catfish wants one, too.

Cowfish

Let's let them kiss each other,
better them than you!

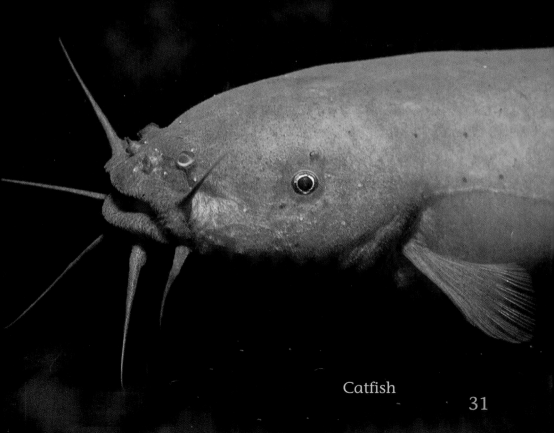

Catfish

Dear Parents:

Congratulations! By sharing this book with your child, you are help-
ing your child become a life-long reader. *Splashy Fins, Flashy Skins* is
perfect for children who are beginning to read on their own. Below are
some ideas for making your child's reading experience an even more
positive one.

Tips for Reading:
- Your child may be able to read this book alone. However, children enjoy reading even more when they read a new book aloud
  with a parent. You might read the first poem and then invite your
  child to read the next poem aloud to you. If your child is unsure
  about a word, ask your child to point to the parts of the word he
  or she knows (your child will likely know the sounds of beginning
  and ending letters and some familiar word parts found in fre-
  quently occurring words). If your child is stumped, read the word
  slowly, pointing to each letter as you sound out the word. Don't
  worry if your child stumbles on words for unfamiliar objects or
  animals. This book is designed to help your child learn new vocab-
  ulary. Always provide lots of praise for your child's hard work.
- *Splashy Fins, Flashy Skins* is written to present your child with inter-
  esting new information. Stop to comment on a fact that is new to
  you. Engage your child in discussion about the book's photographs
  and unusual information as you read together.
- Encourage your child to reread the book again. Rereading, silently
  and aloud, helps children learn to read words more quickly and
  fluently.

Tips for Discussion:
- The title of this book is a real tongue twister. Can the reader come
  up with a different title?

- Moray eels do get their teeth cleaned by shrimp, but there is no
  real Shrimp Salon. Is there anything else in this book that's make-
  believe?

- The backgrounds of many of these photographs are dark,
  because the pictures were taken in the dark depths of the ocean.
  Most of these creatures do not swim where the reader swims. Is
  that a good thing? Which fish would the reader like to have for a
  pet?

Lea M. McGee, Ed.D.
Professor, Literacy Education
University of Alabama